ELEPHANT GOD

LET THE FABLE OF SIX BLIND MEN AND THE
ELEPHANT TEACH US ABOUT GOD

PETER DEHAAN

Elephant God: Let the Fable of Six Blind Men and the Elephant Teach Us About God

Scripture quotations taken from The Holy Bible, New International Version®, NIV®. Copyright © 1973, 1978, 1984, 2011 by Biblica, Inc. Used with permission of Zondervan. All rights reserved worldwide. www.zondervan.com.

Library of Congress Control Number: 2025901918

Published by Rock Rooster Books, Grand Rapids, Michigan

ISBNs:

- 979-8-88809-127-2 (ebook)
- 979-8-88809-128-9 (paperback)
- 979-8-88809-129-6 (hardcover)
- 979-8-88809-130-2 (audiobook)

Credits:

- Developmental editor: Julie Harbison
- Copyeditor: Robyn Mulder
- Cover design: Cassidy Wierks
- Author photo: Chelsie Jensen Photography

To Shara

Series by Peter DeHaan

40-Day Bible Study Series takes a fresh and practical look into Scripture, book by book.

Bible Character Sketches Series celebrates people in Scripture, from the well-known to the obscure.

Holiday Celebration Devotionals rejoices in the holidays with Jesus.

Visiting Churches Series takes an in-person look at church practices and traditions to inform and inspire today's followers of Jesus.

Be the first to hear about Peter's new books and receive updates at PeterDeHaan.com/updates.

CONTENTS

SIX BLIND MEN AND THE ELEPHANT

There is a well-known fable in India about six blind men who encounter an elephant. The men have never seen one and don't know what to expect. When they meet this massive beast for the first time, they rely on their sense of touch to explore the creature and form their understanding of him.

The first man marches forward in confidence and walks into the side of the elephant. With a thump, the man falls to the ground. To him, the elephant is unmovable, a fixed object. He declares that the elephant is like a brick wall. He is not incorrect.

The second man, wanting to avoid what the first

man encountered, is more cautious. He drops to the ground, crawling toward the elephant. When he reaches one of the beast's legs, he wraps his arms around its girth. Unable to make the leg move, he proclaims that the elephant is like a tree trunk. He is not incorrect.

The third man gingerly approaches the elephant with hands stretched out in front of him. The first thing he touches is the elephant's ivory tusk. His fingers explore its formidable length, ending up at the pointed tip. He asserts that the elephant is like a spear. He is not incorrect.

The fourth man, following closely behind the third, cautiously approaches the elephant. He's hesitant. Not wanting to walk into a spear, he stops short. He's curious but wary. The elephant is also curious and stretches out its trunk to touch the man, wrapping his proboscis around the man's arm. The muscular snout surprises the man, and he tries to push it away. He can't. In a panic, he concludes that the elephant is like a snake. He is not incorrect.

The fifth man is much more adventurous than the three who preceded him and not unlike the first. He boldly moves forward and encounters the elephant's side. Unlike the first man, however, he doesn't fall. He gropes his way forward until he reaches the animal's shoulder. That's when the elephant flaps his ears, producing a cool breeze that comforts the man. He states that the elephant is like a fan. He is not incorrect.

The sixth man doesn't take the same path as those who came before him. Instead, he walks toward the animal's hindquarters. The elephant swishes his powerful tail and thwacks the man's shoulder. It stings. He announces that the elephant is like a whip. He is not incorrect.

Each of these six blind men made a reasonable determination about the elephant, comparing the creature to what they knew. Yet each of their assessments is incomplete, laughably so.

Yes, the elephant has the characteristics of a wall, a tree, a spear, a snake, a fan, and a whip. Yet the elephant is so much more.

Even merging these six characteristics into a composite understanding of an elephant still falls far short.

So it is with us and God. As spiritually blind people—at best with spiritually incomplete vision—we can seek to better understand God through word pictures, metaphors, and imagery of what we can comprehend, but we'll still fail to fully grasp what is beyond our comprehension. Still, we're wise to push forward in our quest.

Compare this to working on a jigsaw puzzle. We can hold one puzzle piece and maybe get a hint of what the full picture will look like. Yes, it is a piece of the whole, but it's just a small part of the picture. What we see in that one puzzle piece is reliable, but it's also incomplete.

Now, consider connecting two pieces in our puzzle. Together they represent more knowledge and provide more information than what either can provide alone. More of the picture comes to the forefront. More of it becomes clear, but it's still just a small part of the picture.

Even when we complete our puzzle, we're still looking at a picture, a representation of something far better and grander. At best it's like looking at a reflection in a mirror, where we only know in part (1 Corinthians 13:12).

For now, accept that we'll never fully understand who God is as long as we're here on earth. Though we can understand a part of who he is, we'll never fully comprehend him. Even so, we must embrace all the individual pieces to move toward the completion of the puzzle and gain a more comprehensive idea of who God is and how we relate to him.

In this book, we'll explore many biblical characteristics of who God is. In doing so, we'll move forward to better comprehend the incomprehensible. Though our conclusions will still fall short, they will draw us closer to the Almighty God as revealed to us in Scripture.

Some of these metaphors of God specifically address one part of his being: God the Father, God the Son, or God the Holy Spirit. Others are inclusive, applying to all parts of the Trinity. We'll organize our discussion of these godly metaphors accordingly, all the while expecting to see overlapping characteristics between each part of the godhead. We should not let this trouble us and instead marvel at the wondrous complexity of who God is.

As we do so, some of these word pictures of who he is will resonate with us powerfully. Others will give us pause or even cause consternation. But don't be distressed by that. Each image moves us closer to a holistic understanding of the brilliant mystery of the all-powerful God who created us and wants to be in a relationship with us.

May these scriptural images of God produce

awe and admiration, moving us into a deeper appreciation of him.

Questions:

- Do you think of yourself as being spiritually blind?
- How do you view God today?

FATHER GOD

We read about God throughout the Bible, and he is the focus of the Old Testament. In the New Testament, God sends his Son to earth to save us.

Part of our salvation through Jesus restores us into a right relationship with his Father. Then we can walk with God and connect with him on a personal level, just like Adam and Eve did in the garden of Eden (Genesis 3:8).

Questions:

- What do we think about Father God?
- How do we relate to him?

The term God *can refer generically to our supernatural creator and divine ruler or specifically to the first person of the Trinity. As we continue in this book, we'll use* God *to refer collectively to the Trinity and* God the Father *to mean the first part of it.*

GOD IS OUR FATHER

Over forty times in the Bible, Jesus—whom we'll later see is the Son of God—refers to God as "my Father" (Matthew 7:21, Luke 24:49, John 10:17–18, and many more).

Furthermore, Scripture says that Jesus is God's *only* Son (John 3:16, 1 John 4:9, and others). Yet if Jesus is God's only Son, how can we also be children of God (Matthew 5:9, John 1:12, and Romans 8:14)? How can God also be *our* Father (Matthew 6:9, Romans 1:7, and James 1:27)?

Paul teaches that when we put our faith in Jesus, we become children of God (Galatians 3:26). But how does this make us children of God?

Jesus talks often about the groom (bridegroom)

and his bride, implying that he's the groom, and his followers are his bride.

John the Baptist testifies that he came to pave the way for the Messiah: Jesus, the bridegroom. The bride belongs to the groom (John 3:27–29).

The apostle John reinforces this in his vision of the future wedding of bridegroom and bride (Revelation 21:2, 9). Jesus is the Lamb, and we are his bride.

As the bride of Christ, we become children of the Father through our marriage to his Son. This makes us children of God.

The idea of being spiritually married to Jesus, however, is hard for many people to accept, especially men. Fortunately, there's another explanation that's easier to grasp. It's our relationship with Father God through adoption.

Paul writes that by receiving God's Spirit we're adopted into God's family, becoming his sons and daughters. Through God's Spirit, we can call him, "Abba, Father" (Romans 8:14–15). Being adopted as his sons and daughters was God's plan from the beginning (Ephesians 1:4–6).

Adoption is a beautiful image. As adopted children, God selects us; we're chosen. The act is intentional. Through adoption we become God's heirs, co-heirs with Jesus (Romans 8:16–17).

In both ways, God is our Father. Through our spiritual marriage to Jesus, we become children of God. Through our spiritual adoption into his family, we likewise become his children. As God's children we are heirs of all he has. This includes the inheritance of spending eternity with him (Titus 3:7).

Some people, however, struggle with this imagery of God as our Father because they didn't have good earthly fathers.

Maybe they had an abusive dad or an absent father or a man who didn't pay child support. Their dads may have been selfish, mean, or distant. These men didn't model our heavenly Father to their kids.

Maybe their dad is dead, or they never met him. Perhaps they don't even know who their father is. Or they could have grown up with a less-than-ideal stepdad.

Because of their earthly fathers who were so terrible to them, these children struggle to have a positive view of their Heavenly Father.

I'm grateful that I had a good earthly dad. His example, while far from perfect, made it easy for me to understand what my Heavenly Father is like.

Through my dad, I could readily understand how God loves me, how God cares for me, and how God wants the best for me.

Given my experience, I need to remind myself that not everyone had a father like mine, one who modeled what a good father is like.

All parents have weaknesses; they have faults. They make mistakes. But a good father (and a good mother) will make it easier for their children to see God as a good Father in heaven.

For those whose father's behavior makes it difficult to embrace a Heavenly Father, try to see him as how your earthly father *should* have acted, not by how he was.

Envision him as being kind and loving. He wants what's best for us, and he provides it. That's what our Heavenly Father does for us.

Consider the father in the parable of the prodigal son (Luke 15:11–32). The younger of the two sons demands his inheritance while his dad is still alive. The father gives him what he requests. Then the boy leaves home and squanders his money in wild living. Soon everything is gone. He's broke and starving. Then he remembers the provisions his father's hired men enjoy. He returns home, planning to beg for his father to give him a job.

But he never gets to ask because his dad is watching for his boy to return. When he spots him in the distance, he runs up to him, full of joy, and embraces his boy. He throws a grand party.

So it is with our spiritual Father. Even when we disrespect him, turn from him, and run away, he watches for us to return. He waits. When we do, he'll welcome us back, throw a party, and reinstate us as his child.

With God as our Father, we see him as wise. He's someone we can go to for advice and for help. He lovingly disciplines us when we need it. Father God is also patient with us and loves us unconditionally.

He is the perfect dad.

Questions:

- How did your father point you to God as your Father?
- If areas where your dad faltered make it hard to trust your Heavenly Father, what should you do to correct your image of God as your Father?

FATHER GOD IS THE GARDENER

John records an interesting teaching from Jesus. In this, we get two metaphors for God from one lesson. Jesus says he is the vine, and the Father is the gardener (John 15:1–17). We'll talk about Jesus as the vine in the next section. For now, let's focus on the Father as our gardener.

Just as a gardener prunes a vine or fruit tree to produce quality fruit, Father God prunes us so that we may bear more fruit and better fruit. It may seem counterintuitive to cut off branches to produce a greater yield, but through pruning, the remaining branches produce more fruit of a higher quality.

As our gardener, the Father wisely prunes us in love, knowing what is best for us and enabling us to more fully honor him. Though the process of being pruned may be painful and difficult for the short term, it's necessary for our growth and development. Because of the Father pruning us, we'll produce more fruit and live a life of increased kingdom impact.

Integral to us being pruned by the gardener is that we remain attached to the vine—that is, to stay connected to Jesus. Apart from him we can do nothing.

A related lesson comes from Jesus's parable about the fig tree. The owner looks for fruit on it and finds nothing. Discouraged at being disappointed for three years, he tells the man in charge of the vineyard to cut it down. The man asks for one more year. During this time, he'll give it extra attention: he'll cultivate it and fertilize it. If it produces fruit the next year, great. If not, he agrees to let the owner cut it down (Luke 13:6–9).

It would be incorrect to equate the gardener in this parable with the Father as our gardener. Instead, the owner of the vineyard is the Father, while Jesus is the gardener. Jesus intercedes on

PETER DEHAAN

behalf of the fig tree, and the Father grants it a one-year reprieve.

Though Father God is patient, he's not endlessly tolerant. His grace is not boundless but has limits. In the Old Testament, God was patient with the nations of Israel and Judah for centuries. But eventually judgment came. It was inevitable. He had repeatedly warned them over the years through the prophets. God's judgment will likewise befall us if we continue to be unproductive.

Therefore, it's critical for us to produce fruit to be of use to God. Given this, we will do well to let the gardener—in this case, Jesus—work with us to help us produce fruit.

Even more convicting is another of Jesus's teachings. He says that every tree that fails to produce good fruit will be cut down and burned. Notice the use of the word *good* in this teaching. It reminds us it's possible to produce bad fruit. May we avoid producing bad fruit and instead only produce what is good (Matthew 7:17–19).

Viewing the Father as our gardener, we'll do well to embrace his actions when he prunes us. He does so not as punishment but out of love to help us be as productive as possible. We should cooperate with him in this effort, knowing that he expects us to produce good fruit for him and his kingdom.

Questions:

- What do we think of Father God pruning us?
- Are we producing as much fruit as we can?

FATHER GOD IS THE POTTER

G od is the potter, and we are the clay (Isaiah 64:8). This metaphor of the potter and the clay is a powerful image used in the Bible to illustrate God's role as our creator and the authority he has over our lives. Just as a potter molds clay into various vessels, God shapes us according to his will and purpose.

Some clay is easily moldable. The potter can work with this clay, making it into whatever he wants it to be. It may be something large or something small, something for grand purposes or something for simple uses. The key is that the clay yields to the potter's hand according to the creator's will, purpose, and design.

Yet not all clay behaves like this; it doesn't cooperate. Some clay is not ready for the potter. This occurs if the clay is too dry or too wet. To become usable, the potter sets it aside for a time.

If clay is too hard, it can't be shaped. The potter adds water to it, seals it in a bag, and sets it aside until it becomes soft enough to be molded.

The other extreme is clay that's too soft. It won't hold a shape, and the potter can't use it either. He must also set it aside and give it time to dry out a bit before he attempts to use it.

There may be times in our lives when we feel like we're on the shelf, waiting for God to use us according to his ideal timing. This means we're not ready, and we need to wait. Though God is patient with us, we are often impatient with him. We tire of waiting and push forward on our own, without the potter's hand to prepare us for service.

Instead, we must be moldable and submit to God's plan for us, knowing that he has created us uniquely for his purpose. It may be challenging to accept God's sovereignty in this. Yet as we come to understand and respect it, we can appreciate how he has made us and wants to use us for his glory. Ultimately, we're reminded that God's plan for us is better than ours. We must trust in him and embrace his goodness of having the perfect plan for our lives.

The prophet Isaiah talks about Father God as the potter and his people as clay in other passages too. It's foolish for clay to deny that the potter formed it into the vessel it's become (Isaiah 29:16). The clay does not know better than the potter and should not question what the potter does (Isaiah 45:9).

Jeremiah likewise talks about the authority of God, using the imagery of clay in the potter's hand (Jeremiah 18:6). As our creator, God can do with us what he wants. We can choose to accept that, or we can fight against him.

In his letter to the Romans, Paul confirms God's right over his clay. He can make some vessels for special occasions and others for everyday use (Romans 9:21).

Though God is all-powerful, he also gave us free will. This means we can choose to cooperate with him or oppose him. It's our decision.

As our potter, Father God is like an artist. He molds us into what he wants us to become to accomplish his purpose. This will best grow his kingdom.

For our part, we must be moldable. We must be open to conform to his will and pleasure. This is the best perspective to have as clay in the hands of the potter.

Questions:

- Are we willing to let Father God mold us into what he desires?
- If we feel like God has us sitting on the shelf, what should we do about it?

FATHER GOD IS AN EAGLE

Despite forty years of faithful service leading God's chosen people, God prohibits Moses from entering the promised land. This is all because of a single act of disobedience. This one action is enough to keep Moses from realizing the reward he desires. Even so, he maintains his focus on and reverence for God. With Moses's life winding down, he shares a song with the people and leaves them with a spiritual legacy.

In this song, he says God is like an eagle.

An eagle is a majestic bird. With powerful wings, eagles soar through the air. Seemingly without effort, they glide from one air current to another as they survey their domain and search for food. Eagles build large nests in high places, keeping their young safe from predators.

Speaking specifically of Jacob, and offering us encouragement today, Moses lists four actions of the eagle in caring for its young (Deuteronomy 32:10–12).

These reflect God's character and how he esteems us.

First, the eagle stirs up its nest. Though the verb *stirs* seems confusing in this context, consider the word's ancillary meanings: to cause to become active or to provoke or incite. This action on the nest rouses the eaglets, promoting them to leave the nest and fly—or attempt to fly. I most appreciate this rendering of Moses's words: "As the eagle enticing her young to fly" (Deuteronomy 32:11, DRA).

As an eagle, Father God wants us to grow up, leave the comfort of our childhood home, and fly. He prompts us to do so.

Second, the eagle hovers over its young. It stays nearby; it watches. The parent remains vigilant for the fledgling's first attempt at flight. It doesn't have a hands-off attitude, letting its offspring succeed or fail on its own. The parent instinctively knows these young birds will need help in learning how to fly—and is ready to help, but not until needed.

In the same way as this eagle, Father God remains nearby. He watches us and is vigilant. He knows we'll need his help when we move into what he calls us to do, to metaphorically fly, to take a step of obedience.

Third, the eagle stretches its wings to catch the eaglets as they fall. Though they might accidentally tumble from the nest before they are mature enough to fly, it's more likely that their first attempt at flight will be unsuccessful. That's okay. Their parent is there to swoop down and catch them as they plummet toward earth, saving them from disaster and death.

Like an eagle, Father God catches us when we fall. God had earlier reminded Moses that he did this exact thing for his people (Exodus 19:4).

Fourth, after catching them when they fall, the eagle carries their young aloft so they can try again. Notice that the eagle does not return the fledgling to the nest. Instead, the wise parent prepares them to try again. And again and again—until they succeed.

In similar fashion to the eagle, Father God will

work with us until we can fly on our own—until we succeed.

In these four ways, Father God is an eagle to us.

Questions:

- Which of the four actions of an eagle fills us with appreciation for our Father?
- How should we respond if any of these eagle attributes frustrate us?

FATHER GOD IS OUR REFUGE

Another metaphor for God is that he is our refuge (Nahum 1:7). A refuge is a place of protection that shelters us from danger or hardship. It's a safe place. The idea of God as our refuge occurs throughout the Old Testament in scores of passages spanning over a dozen books. It shows up most often in Psalms, many of which were written by David (Psalm 9:9, Psalm 14:6, Psalm 31:4, and many more).

David rightly sees God as his refuge. Both before he was king, and during his reign, David certainly endured hardships and struggled at many points. Each time, he turned to God and sought refuge in him.

God protected him and provided for him, keeping him safe.

Sometimes this refuge was spiritual and other times it was physical. The physical manifestation of David's refuge was a stronghold. A stronghold is a fortified place or a fortress. David sometimes retreated to a stronghold when threatened or attacked (1 Samuel 23:14 and 2 Samuel 5:17).

In some of his psalms, David mentions both refuge and stronghold in the same thought (such as Psalm 9:9, Psalm 18:2, and Psalm 144:2).

David wasn't the only one, however, to seek sanctuary in strongholds. Prior to David, the people sought strongholds during the time of the Judges (Judges 6:2).

The prophets also talk about the strongholds. Their messages, however, are often ones of warning. In God's judgment, he'll break down strongholds, usually of their oppressors (such as in Isaiah 31:9, Jeremiah 48:41, and Ezekiel 19:7). But it also reflects judgment on God's people (Amos 3:11). Yet other prophecies proclaim protection (Joel 3:16).

The first mention of a refuge occurs in the law of Moses. There God instructs his people to establish cities of refuge when they take the promised land. These cities of refuge would be for people to flee to if they accidentally killed someone. While in the designated cities of refuge, they couldn't be harmed. This would preserve their life to give them the opportunity to stand trial (Numbers 35:9–15). These cities of refuge served as their sanctuary.

To round out our understanding of God as our refuge, David writes that God is his rock and salvation, an unshakable fortress (Psalm 62:6). In another of his psalms, David proclaims God is his fortress, stronghold, deliverer, and shield. There he takes his refuge (Psalm 144:2).

Likewise, the prophet Isaiah proclaims the Lord is our sure foundation, a rich store of salvation, wisdom, and knowledge (Isaiah 33:6).

When Moses blesses the tribes of Israel before his death, he speaks of eternal God as a refuge guarded by everlasting arms (Deuteronomy 33:27).

In God we find our refuge and stronghold. He's our rock and fortress, a sure foundation. He holds us in his everlasting arms.

Questions:

- When we're discouraged, attacked, or

tired, do we go to Father God as our refuge?

- What does taking refuge in him look like?

FATHER GOD IS OUR ROCK

Jesus gives us another parable that points us to God. He talks about two types of people who hear his teaching (Matthew 7:24–27).

Some people embrace what he says and put it into practice. They are like a wise person who builds a house on bedrock, a stable and firm foundation. When the rain comes, the waters rise, and the wind blows against the house, it stands firm. It does not fall because it rests on a solid foundation of rock.

Yet other people hear Jesus's words and don't put them into practice. They don't act on what he tells them to do. Though they may store up knowledge in their mind, it means nothing because it doesn't result in action.

Jesus likens them to foolish people who build their houses on sand. When the rain comes, the waters rise, and the wind blows against the house, it cannot stand. It falls with a great crash. What they built doesn't last because it was constructed on an unstable foundation of sand and not rock.

What is this foundation of rock? It's Father God, whom Jesus's words point us to.

He is a sound foundation on which we should build our home if we want it to stand, to last. If we build on any other foundation—such as sand—we cannot expect to prevail against the forces that batter it. Nature will win. Our houses will not.

If we want to build a house that stands strong in the face of adversity, we must build our house on Father God as our rock.

References to God as the Rock fill the Old Testament.

Recall the chapter "Father God Is Our Refuge." Several psalms connect refuge with rock, praising God as a rock of refuge (Psalm 31:2 and Psalm 71:3).

As Jacob's life nears its end, he blesses his boys. He confirms that Joseph persevered because of the Rock of Israel (Genesis 49:24).

Hannah (the mother of Samuel) praises God for

his unique standing, with no one like him and no Rock like God (1 Samuel 2:2).

Over a dozen times, David proclaims God is "my rock" (such as in 2 Samuel 22:2–3, Psalm 18:2, and Psalm 62:2). The sons of Korah concur (Psalm 42:9).

Isaiah instructs us to trust the Lord throughout our lives as a Rock eternal (Isaiah 26:4). He later proclaims there is no other Rock aside from God (Isaiah 44:8).

Including Isaiah, over twenty Old Testament passages reference God as our Rock, that's Rock with a capital R (such as Deuteronomy 32:4, Psalm 19:14, and Habakkuk 1:12).

Father God is our Rock—our firm, stable, and lasting foundation. We can count on him to keep us from succumbing to the forces that batter us and oppose what we do for him.

Questions:

- Have we built our houses on rock or sand?
- If our house crashes, is it the Father's fault or our own?

EMBRACE FATHER GOD

I n this section that considered Father God, we looked at six metaphors that reveal the Father and his character to us.

After establishing that God is our Father, we likened him to a gardener and a potter. He is also an eagle to us. And he is our refuge and our rock.

Questions:

- Which of these metaphors for Father God do we most connect with? What can we do to embrace it more fully?
- Which of these metaphors do we most struggle with? What steps should we take to lessen our apprehension?

SON

Jesus is the Son of God. We typically think of him as the second person of the Trinity.

Jesus is present in the Old Testament, but the New Testament—primarily the four biographies about him—focus on his life and ministry.

Jesus comes to earth as a baby and grows up to save us. He does this when he sacrifices himself. He dies on the cross to pay the penalty that our wrong behavior—our sin—deserves. In doing so, he redeems us to Father God and restores us into a right relationship with him.

When we follow Jesus, we receive eternal life. This eternal life through him begins the moment we say yes to Jesus. This means our eternal life starts here on earth and continues forever in heaven after we die.

Questions:

- What do we think about Jesus?
- How do we relate to him?

JESUS IS THE SON OF GOD

We readily accept that Jesus is the Son of God. The Bible repeatedly confirms this. Luke painstakingly documents the genealogy of Jesus all the way back to the beginning of time. He ends his lengthy list by saying ". . . the son of Seth, the son of Adam, the son of God (Luke 3:23–38).

The angel Gabriel confirms this when talking to Mary about what will soon take place, of the Holy Spirit supernaturally impregnating her and her giving birth to a holy one, the Son of God (Luke 1:35).

Father God also confirms Jesus as his Son at Jesus's baptism (Matthew 3:16–17, Mark 1:10–11, and Luke 3:21–22). This prepares Jesus for ministry.

Father God does it again when Jesus transfigures before Peter, James, and John (Matthew 17:1–5, Mark 9:2–7, and Luke 9:28–35). Peter confirms he was there (2 Peter 1:17). This occurs toward the end of Jesus's time here on earth and precedes his sacrificial death. In both instances God says, "This is my Son."

Our next confirmation of Jesus being the Son of God comes from an unlikely source. It's the devil. When the devil tempts Jesus, he begrudgingly calls Jesus the Son of God (Matthew 4:3, Matthew 4:6, Luke 4:3, and Luke 4:9).

Other confirmations that Jesus is the Son of God come from Nathanael (John 1:49), demons (Matthew 8:29, Mark 3:11, and Luke 4:41), his disciples (Matthew 14:33), Martha (John 11:27), the demon-possessed man (Mark 5:7), the centurion (Matthew 27:54 and Mark 15:39), and Saul (Acts 9:20).

Jesus himself says he is God's Son (John 10:36 and John 11:4).

If you're male, you know what it's like to be a son. If you're female, you can use your status as daughters to envision sonship.

Either way, we're the biological offspring of two parents. We get our identity from our father and our mother. They nurture us and teach us. They prepare us for the future.

Though human parents are not perfect in how they raise their children, most do so to the best of their abilities and produce good results. Despite their flaws, they help shape us into who we become.

The same is true with Jesus as God's Son. The Father nurtured his Son, taught him, and prepared him for the future—to accomplish his purpose here on earth. More significantly, Father God did this without fault.

Just as Father God was the ideal parent to Jesus, Jesus is the ideal Son. This should fill us with awe when we consider what Jesus did for us when he died for us to make us right with Papa.

In this way, through Jesus, we become sons and daughters of God; we are children of Father God (John 1:12–13, Galatians 3:26–27, and 1 John 3:1). This, too, should fill us with appreciation and with awe.

Questions:

- What do we think about Jesus being God's Son?
- Do we believe and act as though we're sons and daughters of Father God?

JESUS IS OUR SHEPHERD

The word *shepherd* appears throughout the Bible, in both the Old and New Testaments. Some references are to actual shepherds. David's first job before he became king was as a shepherd. Many other Old Testament characters were also shepherds.

Other mentions of shepherds are metaphorical, referring to those who shepherd a flock of people instead of animals. In this way, we sometimes call our spiritual leaders shepherds.

The most profound of all shepherds is Jesus. He is our Shepherd, and we are his sheep.

The apostle John writes that Jesus calls himself the good shepherd (John 10:11). Jesus even gives an extensive teaching on what this means. As our good shepherd, he will watch over us and protect us. We will follow him, and he will keep us safe (John 10:1–18).

The key point is that, as our good shepherd, Jesus is willing to give up his life to save us. In fact, he does just that when he dies on the cross for all the sins we've ever committed or will ever commit. Dying to save another is love at its finest. Through his sacrificial death, we have our sins forgiven and receive eternal life—which starts now here on earth.

Not only is Jesus the good shepherd, he's also the Chief Shepherd (1 Peter 5:4). When the Chief Shepherd appears, we'll receive our everlasting crown of glory.

But even more so than being the good shepherd and the Chief Shepherd, Jesus is also the great Shepherd (Hebrews 13:20–21). As our great Shepherd, he gives us good things so that we may do his will and please him with our work.

This means that as our shepherd, Jesus is the good shepherd, the Chief Shepherd, and our great Shepherd.

As a shepherd, he cares for us. He watches over us. And he protects us. Ezekiel prophetically sees this many centuries before Jesus (Ezekiel 34:11–12).

It's such a comforting image to know that Jesus is our shepherd. He will keep us safe from harm.

As we've mentioned, if Jesus is our shepherd, that means we're sheep. That doesn't excite me as much as in knowing that Jesus is my Great Shepherd.

If you've heard many sermons that mention sheep, you've probably learned that sheep aren't very intelligent animals. In fact, they're rather stupid. I once asked a friend who raises sheep, "Are sheep really as dumb as ministers say they are?"

"No," he answered. "They're worse."

He shared that it's common for a sheep to stick their head through an opening in a fence or gate. Then they think they're stuck. They don't realize they can take two steps back and get out. They assume they're caught in a trap. The poor sheep stands there and baas until someone rescues it . . . or until it dies.

Sheep aren't smart enough to realize how to get out of the messes they get themselves into. That's why the farmer carefully watches his sheep, ready to help them because they're always doing dumb things and getting into trouble.

Jesus does that for us too. He watches us carefully, ready to help us when we do dumb things and get into trouble. As a follower of Jesus, I don't so much appreciate the analogy that I am a sheep. I'd like to think I'm a bit smarter, but I also do foolish things and get myself into trouble. Then I need Jesus to rescue me.

As we mentioned, David began life as a shepherd before he became king. As the youngest son, he was stuck watching over his family's flock of sheep, while his brothers did more exciting things. Yet, his time as shepherd prepared him to lead God's people, first in battle and later as king. It also influenced some psalms he wrote, most notably Psalm 23, which opens with the comforting phrase "The LORD is my shepherd; I shall not want" (KJV). (To contemplate this in depth, read the profound book *A Shepherd Looks at Psalm 23* by W. Phillip Keller.)

There are many other notable shepherds in the Bible. The first one was Abel. Abraham, Lot, and Moses were also shepherds. So, too, were Isaac, Rachel, and Jacob.

The prophet Amos was a shepherd before God called him. Not surprisingly, a reference to shepherds occurs in his writing (Amos 3:12).

Though not shepherds by trade, the prophets

Jeremiah, Ezekiel, Zechariah, and Isaiah mention shepherds even more.

Jeremiah quotes the Lord as saying that he will not run away from being our shepherd (Jeremiah 17:16). He will not flee when danger comes. He will stand firm and protect us. We can depend on him as our shepherd.

Ezekiel likewise quotes God as saying he'll look after his sheep just as a trustworthy shepherd looks after the animals in his care. God, as our shepherd, will rescue us from all the places we wander (Ezekiel 34:12). He will give us one shepherd, through David, who will tend to us (Ezekiel 34:23).

Most of Zechariah's mentions of shepherds are to human shepherds and their failure to care properly for the people. Yet Zechariah first gives a most inspiring prophecy. He looks forward to Jesus as a shepherd who will one day come to save his flock (Zechariah 9:16).

Isaiah writes that we've all wandered off, just like sheep. We've gone our own way. That is, we sin. But God will place all sins, for all people, on the coming Savior (Isaiah 53:6).

Quoting another prophet, Micah, Matthew writes that God will send to his people someone to shepherd them (Matthew 2:6, quoting Micah 5:2 & 4).

Jesus later says, "My sheep hear my voice and listen to me. I know them; they follow me. Through me, they'll live forever, and no one can take them from me—nor can anyone take them from my Father, who is even greater" (John 10:27–29).

Last, we see Jesus as our shepherd confirmed in John's future-focused vision. He writes that Jesus (the Lamb) will sit on the throne and be the people's shepherd. He'll lead them to living water (Revelation 7:17).

Questions:

- Do we trust Jesus as our shepherd?
- What do we think about ourselves being like foolish sheep who get into trouble and need rescuing?

JESUS IS THE GATE

I n our discussion of Jesus as our shepherd, we looked at what he said about himself in John 10:1–18. In this passage, he calls himself the good shepherd. He also calls himself the gate. How can he be both the shepherd and the gate? Which is it?

These are interesting questions, but as our all-powerful, all-knowing God, he can simultaneously do both.

An image, however, that helps me better understand this is to envision Jesus—as the good shepherd—sleeping in the entrance of the sheep pen. In this way, the shepherd also serves as the gate. As the gate, the good shepherd keeps his sheep in and evil out.

As our gate, Jesus keeps us safe.

Yet to stay safe, we must remain in the sheep pen. The pen isn't to restrict us; it's to protect us. Never forget this truth. If we wander off, we leave the safety of the sheep pen behind us. Then the gate can no longer keep us secure from evil.

To continue the metaphor of Jesus as the gate, the only time we should leave the sheep pen is when we follow him. He takes us out to the pasture so we can graze. We recognize him and follow his voice. When we hear other voices call us—worldly distractions and temptations—we don't follow those voices. We don't recognize them—or at least, we shouldn't.

As we head to the pasture and while we're there, he'll watch over us and keep us safe. When we're done grazing, he'll lead us back to the sheep pen. Again, we follow his voice. Once we're safely inside the sheep pen, Jesus—as both our shepherd and our gate—will keep us secure and under his protection.

This beautiful imagery gives us comfort and confidence in our Savior's provision of safety.

Now let's expand this idea of a gate to that of a door. Just as with a gate, a door separates what is inside from what is outside.

Jesus teaches his disciples that prayer is like

knocking on a door. When we knock, the door will open. When we ask, we will receive. When we seek, we will find. Yet we must first ask (Luke 11:1–13).

In the gospel of John, Jesus repeatedly says that we are to ask in his name, and he will do it (John 14:13–14 and John 16:23–24). Asking in Jesus's name is like knocking on his door. He'll open the door and let us in.

Yet the imagery of knocking on the door has another meaning to it. In Revelation, Jesus says that he stands at our door. He knocks. If we hear him and open the door, he'll enter and fellowship with us (Revelation 3:20). Though he wants to be in a relationship with us, it's up to us to decide. We can keep him out, or we can let him in.

When Jesus comes knocking on our door, may we let him in.

Questions:

- Do we recognize Jesus's voice when he calls?
- Have we let Jesus into our lives?

JESUS IS THE LAMB

As we wrapped up our discussion in "Jesus Is Our Shepherd," we said he's both the Lamb and the shepherd (Revelation 7:17). How can he be both? For a moment, let's accept that he is simultaneously both the Lamb and our shepherd, just as we acknowledged he is both the good shepherd and, at the same time, the gate to the sheep pen.

Recall that as our good shepherd, Jesus is willing to die—to lay down his life—to protect his sheep (John 10:11). He will sacrifice himself to save us.

In the Old Testament, a common sacrifice was a lamb. So Jesus (as the good shepherd) sacrifices himself (as a lamb) to save us. It's a beautiful connection between the Old Testament and the New.

Interestingly, Jesus says that as our shepherd he will lay down his life—sacrificed as a lamb—for us. This means that Jesus is first Shepherd and then the sacrificial lamb. In John's epic revelation, however, he switches the order. Jesus is first the Lamb and then becomes the shepherd.

Though this is perplexing for us to grasp, remember that God exists outside of the time-space reality he created for us to live in. Though time matters to us, it isn't an issue for him. Therefore, it's no problem for Jesus to be our shepherd who will later die for us, while also the sacrificial Lamb who will later become our shepherd.

In the New Testament, John the Baptist declares Jesus is the Lamb of God (John 1:29 and John 1:36). The book of Revelation frequently calls Jesus the Lamb, starting in Revelation 5:6–8 and culminating in Revelation 22:1–3, the concluding chapter of John's vision.

The Old Testament prophets of Isaiah and Jeremiah both foresee Jesus as the sacrificial lamb (Isaiah 53:7 and Jeremiah 11:19). Yet we see another allusion to this much earlier, in the book of Genesis.

When God commands Abraham to sacrifice his only son, the patriarch intends to do just that (Genesis 22). As he takes Isaac to the place where they will offer the sacrifice, the son asks the father, "Why aren't we taking a lamb with us to offer as the burnt offering?"

Abraham simply answers, "God himself will provide the lamb." Isaac accepts his father's answer.

When they reach their destination, Abraham builds the altar and lays the wood on it. He binds Isaac and places him on the altar. With knife drawn, he's ready to kill his son. But God intervenes and stops Abraham. It was just a test of Abraham's willingness to obey God, and he passed.

Then Abraham spots a ram caught in the thicket. He catches the ram and sacrifices him in place of his son. In this way, God indeed provided the animal for the burnt offering.

A ram is a male sheep, implicitly a mature one. A lamb is a young sheep, a baby. Though you may assume that a ram and a lamb are close enough—and it's a matter of semantics—I do not. I make a distinction.

Abraham specifically said God himself would provide a lamb, not a ram. What happened?

Jesus is the Lamb of God, but Scripture never

calls him "the ram of God." In this way, we see Abraham's proclamation of God's provision being fulfilled right away, as well as centuries later. God provides a ram for Abraham and a lamb for us—the Lamb of God.

Though Abraham didn't need to sacrifice his only son, God did.

Jesus—as the Lamb of God—becomes the perfect sacrifice for us. He dies so that we may live.

Questions:

- How well do we do at seeing Jesus as a lamb?
- Though the sacrificial lambs in the Old Testament had no choice in being sacrificed, Jesus willingly did. How can we praise him for being our sacrificial Lamb?

JESUS IS OUR SAVIOR

As the Lamb of God, Jesus dies for our sins—he saves us—so that we may reconnect with Father God and live in community with him, both now and forever. This means that Jesus is our Savior.

Fourteen of the psalms anticipate and celebrate the Savior. David asks for his Savior to come quickly (Psalm 38:22). Asaph calls out for the Savior's help for the deliverance from—and forgiveness of—sins (Psalm 79:9). And the sons of Korah plead for restoration through the Savior (Psalm 85:4).

The Old Testament prophets also look forward to the coming Savior who will save them. Isaiah leads all the prophets with ten references. Notably he writes that God proclaims, "See, your Savior comes!" (Isaiah 62:11).

Next comes Jeremiah with three verses about God as Savior. In one of them, God declares that one day salvation will come from one called "The LORD Our Righteous Savior" (Jeremiah 33:16). This is a powerful name packed with meaning.

Hosea also quotes the words of God, commanding the people to acknowledge only one God and Savior (Hosea 13:4). Micah pledges to watch, hope, and wait for the Savior (Micah 7:7). As Habakkuk prays, he proclaims joy in God as his Savior (Habakkuk 3:18).

Mary is the last to add her praise for the expected Savior. Only months before Jesus's birth, Mary says that her spirit rejoices in God her Savior (Luke 1:46–47).

The psalmists proclaim God as Savior and the prophets foresee it. Multiple people, from different times, all celebrate the coming Savior.

As our Savior, Jesus rescues us from the curse of sin to free us so we can embrace everlasting life with him and through him.

Another word for Savior is *Messiah* (Luke 2:11), which means Christ (John 1:41 and John 4:25).

Jesus is our Savior and our Messiah. He is the Christ.

Questions:

- How well do we do at embracing Jesus as our Savior?
- What should our response be to him saving us?

JESUS IS OUR HIGH PRIEST

I n the Old Testament, God implements the priesthood. It starts with Aaron. The people can't approach God directly, but Aaron represents them to the Almighty. Effectively he serves as a liaison between the people and God. In this way, Aaron becomes our first high priest. The priesthood transfers to his sons and then to their sons, generation after generation.

God also gives Moses instructions about the tabernacle, which later transfers to the temple. The people view the tabernacle and then the temple as God's dwelling place here on earth.

Though we get a sense of these things from various Old Testament passages (such as Leviticus 4 and Leviticus 16), clarity emerges from the book of

Hebrews. In this letter, the writers painstakingly connect their New Testament faith with Old Testament practices. It's an insightful explanation that amplifies our understanding of God and our relationship to him.

In the temple is a Holy Place. Behind it is the Most Holy Place (also known as the holy of holies). Only the high priest can enter the Most Holy Place and then just once a year (Hebrews 9:6–8). It's the high priest's role to offer sacrifices for sins (Hebrews 5:1 and Hebrews 13:11).

Jesus comes to be our high priest (Hebrews 8:1–2). As the ultimate high priest, he fulfills the Old Testament's expectations for the position. Yet he doesn't offer an animal sacrifice for the people's sins. Instead, he sacrifices himself (Hebrews 9:11–14) as a final sacrifice to end all sacrifices (Hebrews 9:24–26). Jesus is the perfect sacrifice: holy, pure, and blameless (Hebrews 7:26). Through his sacrificial death as our high priest, he makes us right with Father God.

When Jesus dies, the curtain in the temple that separates the Most Holy Place from the Holy Place rips apart, from top to bottom (Matthew 27:50–52 and Mark 15:37–39). This symbolically allows us direct access to God.

Through Jesus as our high priest, he offers the last sacrifice we'll ever need. This makes us right with Papa and gives us direct access to him. Though Jesus is the intermediary that makes it happen, once he completes his mission, we no longer need someone to approach God for us (Hebrews 4:16). We can do that ourselves because of Jesus, our high priest.

Questions:

- What does Jesus being our high priest mean to us?
- How well do we do at approaching God directly without an intermediary, such as a minister or a prophet?

JESUS IS OUR GREAT PHYSICIAN

Jesus came to earth to heal and to save. Two thousand years ago, people embraced him for his healing power but not so much for his saving power. Today it's the opposite. We turn to Jesus to save us but not so much to heal us.

The four biographies of Jesus—Matthew, Mark, Luke, and John—give multiple accounts of Jesus healing people who come to him. Over one hundred verses talk about Jesus healing people, curing them, and dispatching impure spirits. Regardless of what we understand impure spirits to mean, whatever these people's afflictions were, we know Jesus made their lives better. That's what matters.

Given all this, it's not unexpected to embrace Jesus as the Great Physician. Yet he never calls himself a doctor. He does, however, imply that he is one (Luke 4:23). Healing people—physically, as well as spiritually—is what he came to do (Matthew 9:12, Mark 2:17, and Luke 5:31).

Centuries before Jesus's birth, the prophet Jeremiah foresaw the need for a physician (Jeremiah 8:21–22). Jesus arrives to be that physician, to heal the people—both physically and spiritually.

Once Jesus healed them of their ailments, he taught them. With their physical needs addressed, they were willing to listen to him. This is a model we'll do well to follow today: help people with their physical concerns and then talk to them about spiritual matters. This is one way to put our faith into action (James 2:14–16).

Though some conclude that Jesus is no longer in the business of healing people today, remember that God does not change (Psalm 55:19 and James 1:17). This means if he healed people then, he still heals today. If only we will let him.

Though many of us today have access to comprehensive healthcare, not everyone does. For some people, Jesus is the only physician they'll ever see. For the rest of us, perhaps we should seek Jesus first and doctors second, not the opposite.

He is our Great Physician.

Are we willing to turn to him for our healing?

Questions:

- Do we trust Jesus to save us?
- Do we trust Jesus to heal us?

JESUS IS A HEN

Jesus laments for Jerusalem. They killed the prophets sent to warn them. He knows they'll soon kill him too. Even so, he longs to gather them—his children—together like a hen gathers her chicks beneath her wings (Luke 13:34).

Jesus's audience lives in an agrarian society. They readily understand his reference to a hen and her chicks. But not all people today comprehend this imagery. Because it's unfamiliar, it's easy to dismiss the passage and continue reading. But we shouldn't do that.

Like most mothers, a hen is protective of her offspring.

Imagine a bunch of baby chickens. They're

happily going about their day, pecking at the ground for food and chirping with contentment. They know their mother watches over them, and they feel safe—because they are.

When danger threatens, she calls for them, and they run toward her. They scoot underneath her body, and she lowers herself to shield them from danger. They disappear from view, as if they weren't even there.

Sometimes the chicks get startled, even though they're safe. In a panic, they run to their mom for protection. She gathers them under her wings and comforts them. Yet usually she's the one to take the initiative.

Other times she lifts her wings to cover them and protect them from rain. Jesus may have this passage in mind when he laments over Jerusalem, longing to cover them as a hen covers her chicks.

Another way a hen protects her babies is when they huddle close to her at night. The warmth of her body transfers to them. Without her presence, they will get chilled and could die.

When danger approaches, a hen places herself between her chicks and the menace. Acting like a shield, she often rises to scare away predators or lunge toward them to chase them away. She is willing to die to save her babies.

In the same way, Jesus is like a hen to us. He wants to protect us. Jesus keeps us safe and warm. He comforts us. Jesus longs to gather us under his wings like a hen gathers her chickens. He cares for us. He wants to shield us from danger. And when we're scared, we run to him for protection—at least we should.

In parallel fashion to Jesus covering us with his wings, we see Ruth asking Boaz to cover her with the corner of his garment, implicitly to marry her (Ruth 3:9), which we'll address further in the next chapter. In the prophetic words of Ezekiel, we read how God wants to spread his garment to cover the naked body of unfaithful Jerusalem (Ezekiel 16:8).

We need only go to him, and he will care for us. In this, we have the image of Jesus as being expectant. He waits for us to come to him. (Consider Jesus's parable of the lost son, whose father watches in expectant hope for him to return home in Luke 15:11–32. We covered this in "God Is Our Father.")

Jesus does not force us to come to him. He waits for us. He's ready. He wants to wrap his arms around us, to comfort us and keep us safe.

Jesus desires to protect us from harm. He'll

defend us when attacked. He is willing to die for his children, which is exactly what he does when he sacrifices himself on the cross to save us.

Oh, how Jesus yearns to gather his children in Jerusalem, but he cannot. Why? It's because they aren't willing to let him. Jesus called for them to come to him, but most have ignored him. They won't allow him to protect them and keep them safe. He wishes to help them, but they won't accept his offer.

May we not repeat their error. When Jesus calls us, may we run to him and receive his protection— just as chicks run to their mother.

Questions:

- Do we live life with a sense that Jesus is nearby, watching over us?
- How quick are we to run to Jesus for protection?

JESUS IS THE BRIDEGROOM

Jesus refers to himself as our bridegroom (Luke 5:35). We see this confirmed in John's end-time vision (Revelation 18:23). If he is our bridegroom, that means we're married to him.

Being married to Jesus is a hard concept for many people to grasp, perhaps more so for guys who squirm at the idea of wedded bliss with the Almighty. But just because the imagery may initially make us uneasy, we shouldn't reject it. It's important we push past our apprehension to grab hold of this most amazing metaphor because it's biblical truth. In short, we are lovers.

To appreciate this metaphor of Jesus as our bridegroom, we must push aside our temporal, tangible, physical perspective. Instead, we need to embrace being married to Jesus from a spiritual standpoint. Through our supernatural marital union with him, we will encounter spiritual intimacy and ecstasy. We may experience bliss at its finest.

Isaiah writes that just as a bridegroom delights in his bride, so will God delight in us (Isaiah 62:5). If this shocking imagery seems borderline sacrilegious, remember that it's in the Bible. What Jesus wants with us as his bride is for us to experience a perfect, idyllic, holy connection. This suggests spiritual intimacy between us and him. He wants to enjoy spiritual ecstasy with us. And we should desire it too.

As we consider this and attempt to embrace it, be encouraged to realize that Jesus cares so much for us that he wants this type of intimate relationship with us. Who are we to think we can tell him no?

In John's epic revelation, the apostle hears the multitude cry out in jubilation, rejoicing over the imminent wedding of the Lamb and his bride, of Jesus and his church (Revelation 19:7).

This is what we can look forward to when we join Jesus for eternity.

Yet this is not just something for the future. As

we follow Jesus today, we can prepare ourselves now to experience a taste in this world of our future reality in heaven.

Questions:

- Does Jesus being our bridegroom make us uncomfortable?
- What do we think about experiencing spiritual intimacy with Jesus?

JESUS IS THE VINE

I n "Father God Is the Gardener," we covered the first half of Jesus's teaching about the vine and the branches. In this, Jesus says he is the vine and his Father is the gardener who prunes us—the branches—to be more productive (John 15:1–17).

Through this analogy, Jesus emphasizes the importance of remaining connected to him, because apart from him we can do nothing (John 15:5). Just as a branch cannot survive without being attached to the vine, we—as Jesus's followers— cannot thrive without being connected to God through Jesus.

In the same way as a wise farmer prunes branches of a fruit tree to yield more fruit and of a higher quality, God also prunes us—Jesus's branches—to enable us to produce better fruit. In this illustration, Jesus is the life-giving vine to our branches. As long as we remain connected to Him, we can bear much fruit.

We must remain attached to Jesus for the Father to prune us. It hinges with our connection to Jesus, which starts when we follow him.

From a human standpoint, pruning may be painful and challenging, but it's necessary for our growth and development. Just like a branch severed from the tree cannot survive, we cannot live life to the fullest without being connected to Jesus.

Paul takes this analogy of branches one step further. Addressing those who have rejected Jesus, he likens them to branches broken off from the tree (Romans 11:17–21).

Yet there is hope. They can be grafted back into the life-giving vine of Jesus. Then they can receive nourishment and support from him.

This teaches us that there is always hope for those who feel disconnected from Jesus. Just like those who were cut off when they rejected him but were later grafted back into the tree, God can always reconnect us. This provides the nourishment we need to thrive, through Jesus as our vine. We must trust in him and allow him to guide us through the process of pruning and growth.

Let us remember Jesus as the source of our life and power. By remaining connected to him, we can bear fruit and accomplish great things through his strength. Let us embrace the pruning process, knowing it's for our own good—and for God's kingdom.

As branches of the vine, let us strive to stay connected to Jesus and allow him to work through us to produce fruit that will bring glory to his name.

Questions:

- Are we connected to Jesus, like a branch to a vine?
- Do we get our strength and sustenance from him?

JESUS IS THE CORNERSTONE

I n modern building practices, a cornerstone is a decorative element set in a prominent position of a building. It often commemorates the year of construction and possibly the owner of the building. It may be hollow inside and include a time capsule. The cornerstone is not integral to the structural integrity of the building; it's ancillary. This understanding of a modern-day cornerstone, however, does little to illustrate to us who Jesus is.

In ancient times a cornerstone served a more fundamental purpose; it was essential. It was the first piece of a building that was laid. The builders placed the cornerstone with careful intention. Every other element of the construction related to the position of the cornerstone.

If the cornerstone was off, the rest of the building would be off too. If the cornerstone was sound, the rest of the building—which relied on the cornerstone's position—would be strong and lasting.

Jesus is our cornerstone. If we build ourselves on him, we will be sturdy and endure. Yet without him serving as our cornerstone, whatever we construct will not last.

To extend the analogy, Jesus, our cornerstone, sits on a firm foundation of rock. (See "Father God Is Our Rock.") In this way, we depend on Jesus, whose position rests on Father God.

This idea of Jesus as our cornerstone begins with the prophetic message of Isaiah. There he quotes the words of God, who promises to lay a stone in Zion, tested and sure. It's a precious cornerstone. Those who rely on it will have nothing to fear (Isaiah 28:16).

Peter shares this passage—along with others— in his first letter to Jesus's church (1 Peter 2:6). There, Peter calls Jesus the living Stone—that is, a cornerstone come to life. We, as his followers, become his living stones, used in the construction of a spiritual house. There we serve as a holy priesthood to offer spiritual sacrifices to the Father through Jesus (1 Peter 2:4–5).

Paul also calls Jesus the cornerstone: the chief cornerstone. It's as if to say he's the cornerstone of all cornerstones. Don't miss this: *Jesus is the cornerstone of all cornerstones.*

Through Jesus, we are members of his house, built on the foundation of the prophets and the apostles, with Jesus serving as the chief cornerstone (Ephesians 2:19–20).

The psalmist predicts that the stone the builders reject will, in fact, become the cornerstone (Psalm 118:22). Though most of the Jews in Jesus's day rejected him—thereby fulfilling this prophecy—not all did. For them, along with the Gentiles who believed in him, Jesus became the cornerstone of their faith. He remains our cornerstone today.

Jesus quotes this passage from Psalms when speaking to the Jews (Matthew 21:42, Mark 12:10, and Luke 20:17). Peter likewise references this passage when he testifies before the Sanhedrin (Acts 4:11) and again in his letter (1 Peter 2:7).

Peter continues that there's a stone that causes people to stumble, a rock that makes them fall (1 Peter 2:8). In this, he quotes the words of God, which foresee most of the Jewish people rejecting Jesus (Isaiah 8:14).

May we not repeat their error today. May we depend on Jesus as the cornerstone of our faith and of our life.

Questions:

- How have we placed our foundation on Jesus as our cornerstone?
- What does it mean to us that Jesus is the cornerstone of all cornerstones?

JESUS IS OUR KING

Two passages in the Old Testament proclaim Father God as king (Psalm 145:1 and Malachi 1:14). But this does not detract from the fact that Jesus is also our king. Remember that Jesus and the Father are one (John 17:11 and 22). Therefore, what applies to one arguably applies to the other. This means that both the Father and the Savior can be our king.

In the Bible, most of the references to God as our king refer to Jesus. Therefore, we'll focus on Jesus as our king.

In Isaiah's well-known prophecy about the coming Savior, we read he will perpetuate the reign of David, ruling with perfection from when he takes the throne and lasting forever into eternity (Isaiah 9:6–7).

In one of Daniel's visions, he sees Jesus as receiving authority, glory, and sovereign power. All the nations and all the people will worship him. His kingdom will last forever and be indestructible (Daniel 7:13–14).

Note Daniel's mention of sovereign power. As our sovereign ruler, Jesus exercises supreme authority without limit and without end. But we'd be wrong to conclude his sovereignty means that he controls all things. If he did, he'd have to take away our free will. So even though he grants us the ability to make our own choices, that does not detract from his ultimate authority as our sovereign ruler.

Centuries after Isaiah and Daniel, the Magi may have these two passages in mind when they arrive in Jerusalem in search of baby Jesus. They come to King Herod and ask him where the king of the Jews has been born (Matthew 2:1–2).

Some three decades later, Jesus stands trial before Pilate. The ruler asks him, "Are you the king of the Jews?" Jesus confirms he is (Matthew 27:11, Mark 15:2, and Luke 23:3).

Pilate then places a notice on Jesus's cross

proclaiming him as "The King of the Jews" (John 19:19–22).

It's interesting that the distant Magi and the Roman ruler saw Jesus as king, but most of the Jewish people did not.

Paul proclaims Jesus as the King of kings (1 Timothy 6:15), while John's epic end-time vision confirms it (Revelation 17:14 and Revelation 19:16). All of these verses also proclaim him as "Lord of lords."

When we embrace Jesus as our king, we obey him. We follow him. We worship him. In doing so we acknowledge him as the ultimate authority in our lives. There is none greater than he.

May our words and our actions serve as a powerful witness to others that Jesus is our king: the King of kings and the Lord of lords.

Questions:

- What have we done to make Jesus our king?
- How well do we do at celebrating him as the King of kings?

JESUS IS THE WORD

So far, all our metaphors for Jesus have given us images we can see with our eyes. For this one, we'll use a different sense: hearing.

The apostle John begins his gospel of Jesus with lyrical language. When we read it, we must slow down to absorb its profound meaning.

John opens with the phrase "In the beginning." Does this sound familiar? It's the same three words that open the book of Genesis, which talks about the beginning of the world. In this way, John connects Jesus to creation.

John writes that the Word was there at the beginning. The Word was with God. The Word was God. Through the Word, all things came into being. The Word was life and light (John 1:1–3).

To make sure we don't miss his poetic implication, a few verses later, John confirms the Word took on human form to live with us. The Word is the Son of God, and John witnessed his glory (John 1:14). John will later add that Jesus's name is the Word of God (Revelation 19:13).

The creation account repeatedly uses the phrase "And God said." Since John identifies Jesus as the Word and confirms the Word's presence at creation, we can conclude that it's Jesus—as the Word—who utters us and our world into reality. Jesus *is* the Word.

Before Paul's conversion, when he's referred to by his Hebrew name of Saul, he's on his way to Damascus, intent on imprisoning Jesus's followers. A bright light beams from heaven. He hears a voice, which asks, "Saul, why are you persecuting me?"

"Who are you, Lord?" Paul asks.

"I am Jesus."

The words of Jesus come to Paul from heaven. In a literal sense, Jesus is the Word to Paul (Acts 9:1–6).

In Paul's letter to the church in Ephesus, he tells them to put on the full armor of God (Ephesians 6:10–18). The last piece of armor Paul mentions is the sword of the Spirit, which he identifies as *the word of God* (Ephesians 6:17).

Most people understand *the word of God* as a reference to the written Word of God. Yet at the time of Paul's writing, only the Old Testament existed.

An alternate understanding of *the word of God* is to see it as a reference to God's spoken word. Though God primarily speaks to us through the Holy Spirit, might this also be a reference to Jesus as the Word? If so, we can understand Paul's teaching to be an instruction for us to arm ourselves with the very words of Jesus, who is the Word.

As we embrace Jesus as the Word and as the words of God, may we listen to him and do what he says—all of it.

Questions:

- How well do we do at listening to the words of Jesus in Scripture and obeying what he tells us to do?
- Though we can read Jesus's words in the Bible, how open are we to hear Jesus's spoken words to us today?

JESUS IS LIGHT

As John continues his poetic opening to the life of Jesus, we encounter another twist on our word pictures for God. Though our eyes can see this image, our hands cannot touch it.

John the disciple talks about John the Baptist, whom God sent to testify about the light of Jesus. This was so that all people might believe through him. John the Baptist was not the light, just a witness to the light. As the true light, Jesus gives light to everyone in the world (John 1:4–9).

Later, Jesus confirms he is the light. When we follow him, we'll never walk in darkness again. Instead, we'll have the light of life to guide us and illuminate our path (John 8:12). He is the light of the world (John 9:5, John 12:46, and 1 John 1:5).

In "Jesus Is the Word," we talked about Paul's conversion experience. Jesus—as the Word—speaks to Paul from heaven. Accompanying Jesus's words is a bright light. It's the light of Jesus.

Jesus speaks, and Jesus shines—brightly. The intense light of Jesus is so extreme that it blinds Paul for three days until Ananias arrives. Placing his hands on Paul, Ananias restores Paul's sight (Acts 9:3–19).

As the book of Revelation reaches its climax, we get a glimpse into the new heaven and the new earth. The city—the new Jerusalem—won't need the sun or the moon to provide light. God's glory will give all the light we need. The Lamb—that is, Jesus—is the lamp. The people will walk in his light and rulers throughout the earth will come to it (Revelation 21:23–24).

We'll no longer need the sun to give us light because the Son will replace it and outshine it.

May we always walk in the light of Jesus.

Questions:

- When we encounter darkness, how can we turn to Jesus to light our path?
- If Jesus provides all the light we'll need in heaven, how can we tap into his light today?

JESUS IS THE WAY

One time Jesus talks to his disciples about the future (John 14:1–7). He speaks of his Father's spacious house, with space for everyone. He's going there to get their rooms ready. Then he'll come back to get them. He ends with a confusing statement. He says, "You know the way to the place where I'm going."

Thomas asks the question I'm thinking: "But we have no idea where you're going. How can we possibly know the way?"

Jesus answers by saying, "I'm the way, the truth, and the life. No one can come to Papa except through me" (John 14:6).

In this one succinct phrase, Jesus self-identifies as being the way, the truth, and the life.

The Way: First, Jesus is the way to the Father. The only way to reach Papa is to go through his Son. Though the Old Testament had hundreds of laws to guide the people into right living, they still fell short of meeting Father God's exacting expectations. Though they tried to reach him, they couldn't. Every one of them failed to meet the high standards of the Old Testament law.

Jesus comes to offer a better way. He willingly sacrifices himself for us, dying for the penalty our shortcomings demanded. In this way, he becomes the ultimate sacrifice to end all sacrifices, the one the Old Testament sacrifices could only point to.

Through doing so, Jesus is the way to the Father. In fact, he's the only way. He says so.

John the Baptist points people to Jesus (Matthew 3:1–3, Mark 1:1–4, and Luke 3:1–5). In doing so, John proclaims Jesus as the way (John 1:23). Matthew later confirms it (Matthew 21:32).

The prophets, John the Baptist, and Jesus himself all say he is the way.

Given this, it's not surprising when Luke later refers to Jesus's followers as the Way (Acts 9:2, Acts 19:9, and more).

The Truth: Second, Jesus is the truth. Not only does Jesus speak God's truth, but he is also truth.

He's truth personified. Just as we embraced Jesus as the Word a few chapters ago in "Jesus Is the Word," we can likewise embrace Jesus as the truth.

The apostle John mentions truth far more often than any other book in the Bible. In his poetic prose, we can infer that his many mentions of the truth often point to Jesus (John 1:17, John 3:21, John 5:33, and many more). Most significantly, John records Jesus as saying, "You'll then know the truth. This truth will set you free" (John 8:32).

Perhaps most intriguing is when Jesus talks with the Samaritan woman who comes to draw water from the well. He says that true worshipers will worship the Father in the Spirit and in truth (John 4:23–24). If we see Jesus as the truth, then the true worship of the Father comes through the Holy Spirit and Jesus.

The Life: Third, Jesus is the life. We readily see this as eternal life (John 3:14–17 and John 5:24). This eternal life, however, isn't just what happens after we die. This everlasting life through Jesus starts on the day we follow him. It then continues into eternity after our physical bodies die.

Jesus is the bread of life (John 6:35). He is also the resurrection and the life (John 11:25). And we will have life in his name (John 20:31).

Jesus is the way to the Father. He is the truth about salvation. And when we follow him, he is life eternal.

Yes, Jesus is the way, the truth, and the life.

Questions:

- Do we truly believe that Jesus is the only way to the Father?
- How can we more fully celebrate Jesus as the way, the truth, and the life?

EMBRACE JESUS

I n our second section, which considered the Son of God, we explored fifteen word images that reveal Jesus and his character to us.

It's fitting that nearly half of our metaphors relate to Jesus. We opened by affirming him as the Son of God.

Then we embraced him as shepherd, gate, and lamb, with delightful overlapping and interweaving imagery.

Next, we celebrated him as our savior, high priest, and great physician, who both saves us and heals us.

Jesus is also our hen and our bridegroom. He is the vine, cornerstone, and king. Courtesy of the apostle John, we wrapped up by seeing Jesus as the Word, the light, and the way.

Questions:

- Which of these metaphors for Jesus do we most connect with? What can we do to embrace it more fully?
- Which of these metaphors do we most struggle with? What steps should we take to lessen our apprehension?

HOLY SPIRIT

When we read about Jesus in Scripture, we form a mental picture of him. Most of the references we covered about Jesus as the Son of God are visual images. We also have many visual metaphors to help us comprehend Father God. Yet the Holy Spirit is less tangible and more ethereal.

The Holy Spirit is the third person of the Trinity. This doesn't imply he isn't as important, merely that he's listed last.

When Jesus returns to heaven, God sends the Holy Spirit to us. He lives in us and guides us. In this way, everyone who follows Jesus has God the

Spirit inside of them. He teaches us, guides us, and inspires us.

The Holy Spirit is present throughout the Bible, but he becomes the focus in the book of Acts, as he guides Jesus's church.

May we listen to the Holy Spirit's promptings and do what he says.

Questions:

- What do we think about the Holy Spirit?
- How do we relate to him?

HOLY SPIRIT IS OUR ADVOCATE

Jesus tells his disciples that he'll ask Papa to give them another advocate, someone who will help them and be with them forever. This advocate is the Spirit of truth. Jesus continues by saying that the world won't accept the advocate because they can't see him and don't know him. But we do know him. As Jesus's followers, he lives in us (John 14:16–17).

Though many people have heard of Jesus, as well as God the Father, they're unfamiliar with and wary of the Holy Spirit. The Holy Spirit is only real to those who follow Jesus. To the rest, he is an enigma.

Sadly, the Holy Spirit is also an enigma to too

many people who proclaim to follow Jesus. As we consider these facets of the Holy Spirit, may he become more real to all of us—as Jesus's followers —and more active in our lives.

An advocate is someone who represents another of lesser standing to someone of greater standing. They speak on this person's behalf, plead their case, and argue in their favor. Another word for advocate is intercessor; it's someone who intercedes for us.

We read about the Holy Spirit as our advocate elsewhere in Scripture.

A few verses later in John's gospel, Jesus confirms that the Advocate—this time with a capital A—is the Holy Spirit. The Father will send the Holy Spirit in Jesus's name. The Holy Spirit will teach them all things that Jesus had said (John 14:26).

Later Jesus says the Advocate will testify about him (John 15:26).

Then Jesus clarifies that the Advocate cannot come until he goes away. But after Jesus leaves, he will send the Advocate to his followers (John 16:7).

Though we may think it would be better to have Jesus with us than the Holy Spirit, remember that Jesus in physical form can only exist in one place at a time. Therefore, he can only minister to one person or one group of people in that instance. The Holy Spirit, however, doesn't have this limitation. As a full manifestation of God, the Holy Spirit is omnipresent, able to be everywhere at once. In this way, the Holy Spirit can minister to—and advocate for—every one of us, wherever we are.

Though many versions of the Bible use the word Advocate, others use Comforter, Counselor, Helper, Champion, Holy Spirit, and Paraclete (which means Holy Spirit). The Amplified Bible also uses the words Intercessor, Strengthener, and Standby. These compelling terms combine to help us better understand the power and purpose of the Holy Spirit.

May we embrace the Holy Spirit as an ever-present power in our lives who advocates for us. He comforts, counsels, helps, champions, intercedes, strengthens, and stands by us.

These descriptions should give us peace and fill us with confidence, as provided by the Holy Spirit.

Questions:

- How well do we do at embracing the Holy Spirit as our Advocate?

- Which of these synonyms for advocate give us the most insight and clarity about the Holy Spirit?

THE HOLY SPIRIT IS FIRE

The disciples are to stay in Jerusalem and wait for this power from on high, which Papa promised and Jesus will send (Luke 24:49). When this happens they will receive the baptism of the Holy Spirit (Acts 1:4–5).

On Pentecost, which occurs fifty days after Jesus rose from the dead and ten days after he ascended into heaven, his followers gather, meeting in one place. Their numbers have now swelled to 120 (Acts 1:15). There's likely that many present and possibly more meeting on this momentous Pentecost.

That's when Jesus sends them the gift that the Father promised.

They hear a sound like a rushing wind that fills the place. They see what looks like tongues of fire that come to rest on each one of them. The Holy Spirit fills them, and they speak other languages. Bewildered, a crowd of people gather and hear the disciples address them, each one hearing their native tongue. They're both amazed and perplexed (Acts 2:1–12).

Under the power of the Holy Spirit, Peter preaches to the crowd. He connects Old Testament prophecies with what the people are witnessing. He tells them of Jesus's sacrificial death to save them from their sins. Many are convicted. They ask him what to do. He tells them to repent and be baptized in the name of Jesus Christ for the forgiveness of sins and to receive the gift of the Holy Spirit. About three thousand people believe that day and are baptized (Acts 2:14–41).

Notice the two outcomes of repentance: The first is salvation. The second is being filled with the Holy Spirit.

On this momentous day, the Holy Spirit manifests as fire.

John the Baptist foresaw this. He baptized people with water to symbolize their repentance. Yet one coming after him—Jesus—would baptize the people with the Holy Spirit and fire (Matthew 3:11 and Luke 3:16). This happens just as John proclaimed, starting on that Pentecost and continuing for all who follow Jesus.

Though most mentions of fire in Scripture relate to judgment, this time it's different. On Pentecost, fire represents the supernatural power of God, sent by Jesus, as promised by the Father.

Not only does fire provide warmth and comfort, but it's also mesmerizing to watch. So, too, with the Holy Spirit. The Holy Spirit warms and comforts us spiritually. He mesmerizes us and fills us with supernatural power.

Another purpose of fire is to refine us.

We read of this from the Old Testament prophets. God will refine the people like silver and test them like gold. They will call on him, and he will answer. They will be his people (Zechariah 13:9).

Malachi writes that God's messenger will be like the refiner's fire, purifying the Levites who will offer him their righteousness (Malachi 3:1–3). Will he not do the same for us today?

The apostle Peter later writes that our suffering now proves the genuineness of our faith, greater even than gold refined by fire. The result will be praise, glory, and honor to Jesus when he returns (1 Peter 1:6–7).

Finally, to the church in Laodicea, Jesus tells them to buy from him gold refined in fire to become rich (Revelation 3:18). Their purification is an investment in their future.

Through the Holy Spirit as fire, God supernaturally equips us to serve him and refines us to become pure and righteous.

Questions:

- Do we allow the Holy Spirit to warm us, comfort us, and mesmerize us?
- What do we think about the Holy Spirit refining us with fire?

HOLY SPIRIT AS WIND

On that momentous Pentecost, when Jesus sends the Holy Spirit, not only does the Holy Spirit appear as tongues of fire, he also manifests as wind (Acts 2:2).

The wind blows wherever it pleases. We can hear the effects of the wind and see what it does, but we can't see the wind itself. We also don't know where it's coming from or where it's going.

In this way, the Holy Spirit is like the wind. Just as we can't see the wind, we can't see the Holy Spirit. We can sometimes hear the wind and see what the wind does. In the same way, we can realize the impact of the Holy Spirit. Just as we don't know where the wind will go or what it will do, so too with the Holy Spirit (John 3:8).

As wind, the Holy Spirit is a delightful mystery of what is physically invisible but spiritually real. He moves among us unseen. Yet he is also most powerful.

We first read about the Spirit of God—that is, the Holy Spirit—in the creation account. Just like wind, he moves over the waters (Genesis 1:2). He's poised to take part in creation.

Centuries later, after Jesus dies and rises from the dead, he imparts the Holy Spirit on his disciples. He does this by breathing on them. His breath comes out—much like the wind—unseen but able to be felt (John 20:22). In this way, we see the breath of Jesus foreshadowing his sending us the Holy Spirit, which manifests as wind.

Interestingly, John doesn't say that the disciples receive the Holy Spirit when Jesus breathes on them. We might better understand Jesus's actions as preparing them to receive the Holy Spirit after he is gone, which we read about in the book of Acts (Acts 2:1–41).

Just as the wind moves and works in our physical environment, so too does the Holy Spirit function for us in the spiritual realm. In this way, we embrace the mysterious movement of the Holy

Spirit in our lives, allowing him to work in us and through us.

Questions:

- How does understanding the Holy Spirit as being like wind aid in our understanding of him?
- When have we seen the effects of the Holy Spirit's work in our lives?

HOLY SPIRIT AS A DOVE

When John baptizes Jesus, three things happen when he comes out of the water (Matthew 3:16–17).

First, heaven opens. We're left to imagine exactly what this means. Perhaps it's a figurative reference, preparing us for what happens next. Or do the people who witness Jesus's baptism also get a glimpse into heaven? If so, that would be amazing. It later happens to Stephen (Acts 7:55–56), so why not at Jesus's baptism too?

Second, the Holy Spirit descends from heaven like a dove and lands on Jesus.

Third, a voice from heaven booms. "This is my boy. I love him and am well pleased."

In Luke's account of this event, he adds that

before these three things occur, Jesus prays (Luke 3:21–22). From this, we can infer a connection between prayer and receiving the Holy Spirit.

In Mark's gospel account of Jesus, he includes another detail. He says that as soon as the Spirit enters Jesus, he immediately sends Jesus to the wilderness (Mark 1:10–12).

In the desert, Jesus fasts for forty days. This prepares him for ministry. The devil also uses this time to tempt Jesus and distract him from his mission. We get the most details about what happens from Matthew (Matthew 4:1–11).

The book of John gives us a different perspective. In it, the apostle John, who wrote the book, quotes John the Baptist's testimony about the event. Father God had told John the Baptist that when he sees the Holy Spirit descend from heaven and land on a person, that he is God's Chosen One (John 1:32–34). In this way, when John the Baptist sees the Holy Spirit—appearing as a dove—rest on Jesus, John confirms who Jesus is and what he comes to do.

In all four accounts of Jesus's baptism, we see the Holy Spirit descend from heaven in the form of a dove. The dove, which we can see, represents the Holy Spirit, whom we can't see.

When Jesus later sends his disciples out into the world to tell others about him, he tells them to be as innocent as doves (Matthew 10:16). Might this reference to doves be a reminder to go out in ministry under the power of the Holy Spirit?

We often associate a dove with peace. In this way, we see the Holy Spirit coming to us in peace and filling us with peace. Interestingly, when Jesus prepares his disciples to receive the Holy Spirit, the first thing he says is, "Peace be with you!" (John 20:21–23).

Besides being innocent and representing peace, doves are also gentle, friendly, and easygoing. The Holy Spirit is also like that with us.

Most of the Bible's other references to doves don't relate to the Holy Spirit. Still, we'll do well to embrace the Holy Spirit who lives in us as peaceful, gentle, friendly, and easygoing. He reveals truth to us and guides us in what we should do.

Questions:

- Do we perceive the Holy Spirit as peaceful, gentle, friendly, and easygoing?
- How can we better epitomize these four traits in our lives and our actions?

HOLY SPIRIT GIVES POWER

In Scripture, the Holy Spirit is the star of the book of Acts as he leads Jesus's people after he returns to heaven. The rest of the New Testament reflects the work of the Holy Spirit in Jesus's followers.

Yet the Holy Spirit is not only in the New Testament. He also appears in the Old Testament, showing up in over seventy verses. There we read about the Spirit, with a capital S, confirming him as part of the godhead.

Though all of Jesus's followers have the Holy Spirit living within them, this was not so prior to Jesus sending us this gift. In the Old Testament, the Holy Spirit only fills select people, often for a specific instance. There we read about Holy Spirit power coming upon judges, kings, and most notably prophets, among others.

We've already mentioned the Spirit's presence at creation (Genesis 1:2), which Job confirms (Job 33:4). Here are some other selected instances of the Spirit's infilling presence and power in the Old Testament:

During the time of Moses, the Spirit of God prepares Bezalel for work on the tabernacle (Exodus 31:1–5). Later, the Spirit fills seventy men so they can help Moses (Numbers 11:16–17). And Balaam, despite having selfish motivations, also prophesies under the Spirit of God (Numbers 24:1–3).

In the book of Judges, several men move under the Spirit of the LORD's power: Othniel (Judges 3:9–10), Gideon (Judges 6:34), Jephthah (Judges 11:29), and many times for Samson (starting in Judges 13:24–25).

For kings, we have Saul (1 Samuel 10:6–7), but it's short term (1 Samuel 16:14). Most notably is David (1 Samuel 16:13 and 2 Samuel 23:1–2, along with 1 Chronicles 28:12). David writes of the Spirit's power (Psalm 51:11, Psalm 139:7, and Psalm 143:10).

During the time of the kings, we read of the Spirit at work in Saul's men (1 Samuel 19:19–20),

Amasai (1 Chronicles 12:18), Azariah (2 Chronicles 15:1), Jahaziel (2 Chronicles 20:14), and Zechariah (2 Chronicles 24:20).

Last are the prophets. They all function under the power of God's Spirit (Nehemiah 9:30), but for some, we read of specific mentions of being moved by the Spirit.

We start with Isaiah (Isaiah 48:16), who often prophesied about the Spirit (such as Isaiah 11:2, Isaiah 32:14–15, and Isaiah 61:1).

Ezekiel (Ezekiel 2:2 and Ezekiel 11:5) was often transported by the Spirit (such as in Ezekiel 3:14, Ezekiel 8:3, and Ezekiel 11:24). The most well-known occurrence is when he was set in the middle of the valley of dry bones (Ezekiel 37:1).

These instances of physical relocation, however, are not unique to Ezekiel. Phillip is later physically relocated to Azotus after he baptizes the Ethiopian treasurer (Acts 8:39–40). Prior to Ezekiel, the people act as though Elijah had also experienced being physically moved from one place to another by the Spirit of the LORD (1 Kings 18:7–12 and 2 Kings 2:16).

Like Isaiah, Ezekiel also prophesied about the Holy Spirit (Ezekiel 37:14 and Ezekiel 39:29).

The Spirit of the LORD also fills Micah (Micah 3:8).

Joel gives a stirring prophecy about the Holy Spirit being poured out on all people (Joel 2:28–29). Did you catch that? On *all* people.

Other Holy Spirit prophecies come from Haggai (Haggai 2:5) and Zechariah (Zechariah 6:8).

The Holy Spirit gave power only to selected individuals in the Old Testament. This all changed after Jesus returned to heaven and sent us the Holy Spirit—to fill *all* people, which Joel prophesied and Peter confirmed (Acts 2:16–17).

Today, all who follow Jesus have the Holy Spirit living within them. It's up to us to listen to his words and obey what he tells us to do.

Questions:

- How well do we do at hearing and obeying the Holy Spirit?
- How often do we tap into the Holy Spirit's power in our daily living?

EMBRACE THE HOLY SPIRIT

I n this section that considered the Holy Spirit, we looked at five word pictures that reveal the Spirit of God and his character to us.

Though not as numerous or as tangible as the metaphors for Father God and Jesus, we have powerful word pictures that help us better comprehend the Holy Spirit.

As our Advocate, the Holy Spirit is fire, wind, and a dove. He fills us with supernatural power.

Questions:

- Which of these metaphors for the Holy Spirit do we most connect with? What can we do to embrace it more fully?

- Which of these metaphors do we most struggle with? What steps should we take to lessen our apprehension?

MORE METAPHORS

We began this book by looking at several metaphors that reflect Father God to us, illuminating our understanding of who he is and helping us relate to him more fully. Then we looked at even more images that reveal Jesus, his Son, to us. Third, we considered word pictures that helped us better understand the wondrous, unseen work of the Holy Spirit.

At times, the distinguishing lines between these three parts of God blur. Yet we shouldn't let this concern us because each part is one aspect of God.

Now we'll consider some more metaphors that

transcend this distinction and apply to all parts of the Trinity of God the Father, God the Son, and God the Holy Spirit. Scripture doesn't use the word *Trinity*, but the concept of a three-in-one godhead is there (Matthew 28:19).

Though all three parts of God are present throughout the Bible, the Old Testament primarily focuses on God the Father. In the New Testament, the four gospel accounts of Matthew, Mark, Luke, and John focus on God the Son. In the book of Acts, which covers the early church, we see our focus shift to God the Holy Spirit. The Holy Spirit continues to guide Jesus's church throughout the rest of the New Testament and continues to guide us today.

Yet God's three parts are not independent but are interconnected and inseparable.

Though it's often helpful to consider the three parts of God individually, other times it's easier—even preferable—to consider them together in a holistic representation of who God is and how we relate to him.

What follows are metaphors that reveal our amazing, multi-faceted God to us.

Questions:

- What do you think about the Trinity?
- How do you relate to a three-in-one godhead?

CREATOR

Many people esteem Father God as our Creator. Though he is present at creation, he doesn't make us all by himself. We see this confirmed when God says, "Let us make mankind in our image" (Genesis 1:26).

The Holy Spirit is also present at creation, with him hovering over the waters at the very beginning of the week (Genesis 1:2). We touched on this in "Holy Spirit as Wind."

Through the apostle John, we know Jesus is also there at creation and takes part in it. In fact, all things were made through him (John 1:1–4). We mentioned this in the chapter "Jesus Is the Word."

As such, creation emerges as a community effort with all three parts of the Trinity present: Father,

Son, and Spirit. If we attempt to assign roles to creation, we might label Father God as the visionary, the Spirit as instigating it, and Jesus as speaking the words to make it happen. This, of course, is little more than an intriguing conjecture.

Many passages throughout the Old and New Testament confirm God as creating our reality. He makes—or, more correctly—they make us and our world. Lest there be any doubt, Scripture affirms creation as a praiseworthy event (Psalm 148:5–6).

Notably, David celebrates the Lord for creating his innermost being, for putting him together while still in his mother's womb (Psalm 139:13).

The book of Isaiah talks more about what God created than any other book of the Bible (Isaiah 40:26). We should marvel at his creation, as it points us to him (Isaiah 41:19–20). Isaiah also foreshadows salvation for the people the Lord created (Isaiah 43:1–7 and Isaiah 57:16).

In Job's lament over his physical suffering, he still affirms God for making him (Job 14:15) and for his Lord's sovereignty (Job 10:8).

In the New Testament, Paul also acknowledges and celebrates our creation (Ephesians 2:10, Colossians 1:16, and 1 Timothy 4:4).

Later, when this world is no more, God will

create a new heaven and a new earth for all who follow Jesus (2 Peter 3:13 and Revelation 21:1). This new heaven and new earth will emerge as a fresh creation for us—his created—where we'll live with him forever.

As the creator of us, our world, and the surrounding universe, we should praise God for his wondrous handiwork. We must guard against abusing his creation. Instead, we must take good care of it, just as he charged Adam to do in the Garden of Eden (Genesis 2:15).

When we respect God's creation, we respect the Creator.

Questions:

- What can we do to more adequately praise God as our Creator?
- How can we do a better job of taking care of God's creation?

LORD

The word *Lord* appears thousands of times in Scripture, appearing in most every book of the Bible. Some uses of *lord* (with a lowercase l) show respect to other people. But most occurrences of *Lord* (with an uppercase L) reflect our Lord God. Many versions of the Bible note this by sometimes writing it as LORD. The historical reason for this was to denote the name of God (YHWH), which scribes deemed too sacred to speak.

We see both uses in one verse, when David writes, "The LORD says to my lord..." (Psalm 110:1).

In a general sense, a lord is someone of high rank. It could be a king, a ruler over a territory, or even the proprietor of a manor. In more structured societies, lord may be a title or greeting used by one person of lower stature to address a person of higher standing. It could also express humility, using it to elevate the status of the person being greeted over the greeter.

Let's keep these common usages in mind and amplify them in acknowledging God as our Lord.

When we call him Lord, we do so knowing he holds a much greater rank—infinitely so—than we do. We affirm this by calling him Lord. He is our Creator, and we are the created. In the same way, he is our Savior, and we need his salvation.

Most of the occurrences of *Lord* in the Bible appear in the Old Testament and refer to Father God (such as Genesis 6:5, Ruth 4:14, and Jeremiah 1:2, along with thousands more).

In the four gospel accounts in the New Testament, we see many people refer to Jesus as Lord (such as Matthew 8:8, Luke 5:8, and John 11:27).

Jesus also identifies as Lord when he says he's the "Lord of the Sabbath" (Matthew 12:8, Mark 2:28, and Luke 6:5). Beyond this, Paul confirms that "Jesus is Lord" (Romans 10:9 and 1 Corinthians 12:3).

Over one hundred times, the New Testament uses the title "Lord Jesus" (such as in Acts 1:21, Hebrews 13:20, and Revelation 22:20–21). In sixty of these occurrences, the title is further expanded to "Lord Jesus Christ" (Acts 11:17, 1 Corinthians 1:6–8, and 2 Peter 1:16.)

Yet beyond acknowledging Father God as Lord and Jesus as Lord, the Holy Spirit is also Lord. Paul says that the Lord is the Spirit. When the Spirit of the Lord is present, we have freedom (2 Corinthians 3:17).

We rightly and reverently embrace the Father, Son, and Holy Spirit as our Lord. As we do, may we worship and serve our Lord to our fullest.

Questions:

- What can we do to celebrate God as Lord?
- How can we better acknowledge the Holy Spirit as our Lord?

JUDGE

The word *judge* appears over two hundred times in the Bible. Most of these are with a lowercase j, used as a noun to indicate a person who is a judge or a verb to show the act of judging someone. Yet seven times Judge appears with an uppercase J. This reflects God as our Judge.

When Abraham intercedes for the people of Sodom and pleads for them to escape judgment, he calls God "the Judge of all the earth" (Genesis 18:25).

Later, when Jephthah confronts the Ammonites, he defers to the LORD as Judge to decide between him and the Ammonite king (Judges 11:27). When the king ignores Jephthah, the Spirit of the Lord comes upon him, and he defeats the Ammonites.

We see this as God's judgment through his servant Jephthah.

Despite Job's suffering, he maintains his innocence from wrongdoing and pleads with "my Judge for mercy" (Job 9:15). When his ordeal ends, God—as the Judge—blesses Job with twofold of all that Satan took (Job 42:10).

The psalmist asks God to arise as "Judge of the earth" to punish those who oppose his people (Psalm 94:2). It's human nature to want judgment for those who oppose us, but not for ourselves. Then we want God's mercy.

Though judgment may seem like an Old Testament concept, mentions of God as Judge occur in the New Testament too.

The writers of the letter to the Hebrews refer to God as "the Judge of all" (Hebrews 12:23). This confirms that our Judge did not leave after Jesus died for the judgment of our sins but is still present.

Next, James tells us not to grumble against each other or we'll face judgment. Then he warns that the Judge is standing at the door (James 5:9). We should remember this image of judgment standing at our door, especially when we're tempted to grumble.

In writing to his protégé Timothy, Paul refers to

the Lord as "the righteous Judge." The judgment Paul anticipates, however, is not for punishment but for reward (2 Timothy 4:8). In this way, we see a positive side to God as our Judge. May we embrace this perspective.

It's easy to celebrate God as a loving God who offers us grace and mercy. We'll do well to focus on this, but we should balance it with the reality that God is also our Judge.

Yet we need not quake in fear over his judgment for all the wrong things we have done. Jesus died as the ultimate sacrifice for our sins. In doing so, he appeases the judgment of God and makes us right with the Father.

Through Jesus, as our Savior, we have no reason to fear God as our Judge.

Questions:

- If the idea of God as our Judge produces fear and worry, what should we do?
- How well do we embrace God as a Judge who looks for ways to reward us?

CONSUMING FIRE

I n "The Holy Spirit Is Fire" we covered that fire represents the Holy Spirit. Yet fire can also apply to Father God—and perhaps even Jesus—as a consuming fire.

We may grapple to understand what *consuming fire* means. Since we comprehend fire, let's focus on consuming. To consume means to use up, but that understanding does not apply to *consuming*. Instead, *consuming* can mean intense, strongly felt, and overwhelming. These carry worrisome connotations. Yet *consuming* can also mean engrossing, enthralling, and gripping. That's more positive.

But which of these synonyms for *consuming* apply to God as our consuming fire?

Let's consider what Scripture says.

First, God's glory on the mountain looks like a consuming fire (Exodus 24:17). It is intense, even overwhelming—and scary. Though this implies awe, it's more of a fearful—even paralyzing—reverence type of awe.

Next, our Lord as a consuming fire reveals his jealous nature (Deuteronomy 4:24). His passion for us is strongly felt. It comes out as jealousy. In other passages, the Bible confirms him as a jealous God (such as Exodus 34:14 and Deuteronomy 5:9).

Third, David writes a psalm of praise celebrating God's power and deliverance (Psalm 18:8 and also in 2 Samuel 22:9). Again, we get a sense of God as intense.

Isaiah declares God as burning with anger, whose lips proclaim wrath, with his tongue a consuming fire (Isaiah 30:27). This is a raging anger (Isaiah 30:30).

Last, Isaiah speaks of sinners, asking rhetorically, "Who can dwell in his consuming fire, a place of everlasting burning?" (Isaiah 33:14). In this we see God's consuming fire as the eternal judgement of hell. We most definitely want to avoid that.

All these verses about God's consuming fire are cause for concern. From a fearful reverence to eternal damnation, God as our consuming fire is not something to trifle with. Yet these are all Old Testament references.

The New Testament gives a singular verse about God's consuming fire. In Hebrews we see a positive side to it. As Jesus's followers, we receive a kingdom that cannot be shaken. Our response is thankfulness, which results in worship with reverence and awe—because our God is a consuming fire (Hebrews 12:28–29). As our consuming fire, we are engrossed and enthralled in him.

This New Testament verse reflects eternal life and gives us a reason to celebrate God's consuming fire.

Though we have many reasons to fear God as a consuming fire, as his children, we have a much better reason to appreciate him for this trait.

We will be wise to balance these two facets of God's consuming fire.

Questions:

- What does God as a consuming fire mean to us?
- How can we praise God as a consuming fire?

MASTER

When we consider God as our Master, that makes us his servants. Some people embrace this imagery, while others struggle with it.

A master is someone who's in control over a person or group. The master is in charge, and the servants are expected to do what the master says. At least that's what good servants do: they obey.

In extreme situations, the master is the owner of a slave. Though slavery is now illegal, we aren't wrong to extend the concept of obedience to our employers. In a practical sense, our bosses are our masters; we should do as they say—assuming we want to keep our jobs. Of course, if our human masters ask us to disobey God, we must put God first (Acts 5:29).

As dutiful servants, we must be attentive to our master's needs, ready to act. So, too, with us and God (Psalm 123:1–2).

Though I seldom go to one, imagine the scene at an upscale restaurant. A skilled waiter seems to know exactly when we have a need. The moment our water glass is low, he appears, ready to refill it. When we finish our meal and lay down our fork, our plate is swiftly whisked away. Though often unseen, he is always observing, finely attuned to our needs, sometimes before we even recognize them ourselves.

In our relationship with God, we're called to embody this same spirit of attentive responsiveness and service. Like vigilant servants, we must be ever watching for signals from our Master, seeking to discern his will, obey his commands, and serve him with excellence.

This means actively seeking ways to serve, understanding what God desires, and even anticipating his requests before he speaks. Just as a dedicated assistant can foresee a leader's needs and address them, we too must be ever attentive to God's leading in our lives, seeking to assist and fulfill our Master's purposes.

The story of Samuel is a beautiful illustration of this. God calls to the young boy Samuel in his sleep, but Samuel assumes it's Eli—his earthly master— calling him. Each time Samuel hears the voice, he rushes to Eli, asking what he needs. Eli eventually realizes it's God calling Samuel and instructs the young boy to say, "Speak, for your servant is listening" (1 Samuel 3:1–14). The young boy does.

So, too, should be our interaction with God as our heavenly Master. We must listen, respond immediately, and obey without hesitation—just like Samuel did for both Eli and God.

May we be like the faithful servants in Jesus's parables who hear the master's praise, "Well done, good and faithful servant" (Matthew 25:14–26 and Luke 19:11–26).

Sometimes, however, a servant can have dual loyalties. That never works. Jesus says we cannot serve two masters. In his example, he's talking about trying to serve God and money at the same time (Matthew 6:24 and Luke 16:13). Yet the example of splitting our allegiance applies in every situation. God wants us to give him 100 percent, not in partial obedience but in complete dedication.

Also, it's critical to know that the servant is

never above his master, just as a student is not above his teacher (Matthew 10:24 and Luke 6:40). As a servant to the Master, our attitude should be one of humble obedience and not expectant for any reward. We're just doing our duty (Luke 17:7–10).

In all this, it's important to recognize that being the Master's servant is a decision we must make. Our servitude is not involuntary, as with a slave. We possess free will, granting us the freedom to listen to and obey our Lord and Master or to turn away from him and disregard what he says.

Though our Master desires our obedience, he doesn't force our compliance. It's a choice we make. We respond to his love, not out of obligation but a result of appreciation for him and all he's done for us.

How do we know what our Master wants us to do?

It starts with Scripture. We read about the will of the Father and his Son in the Bible. This is the *written* Word of God.

Yet don't overlook the Holy Spirit as our Master too. From him we receive the *spoken* word of God. In this sense, the Holy Spirit can be—should be—an active Master in every aspect of our life.

As our Master, God is in charge; he's the boss.

It's up to us to follow his directives through active listening and faultless obedience.

Questions:

- How well do we do at embracing God as our Master?
- What can we do to better know what our Master wants and to serve him more fully?

FRIEND

The idea of God as our friend can be difficult for some people to grasp—and to embrace. Many people harbor a fear of God, but it's essential to not wallow in it. While we should have a healthy reverence and awe for our Creator, it should never lead us to a paralyzing fear —one that imagines God as a distant figure, waiting for us to falter, only to strike us down or bring us pain. This understanding of God is misguided— and wrong.

For those who struggle with the truth of God as a friend, it often comes from a difficulty to relate to him on a personal level. However, the Bible provides us with profound examples of friendship between God and humanity, inviting us into a closer relationship.

In Scripture we read that God speaks to Moses face to face, just as one speaks to a friend (Exodus 33:11). This passage illustrates a profound intimacy where God engages in direct communication with Moses. It's so extraordinary that the radiance of God's presence leaves Moses's face shining. The people are so overwhelmed by his glow that Moses wears a veil to shield them from his brightness when he speaks to them (Exodus 34:33–35).

Consider what it means to be friends with God. Friendship builds on communication, sharing experiences, and spending time together. Yet we acknowledge that God remains profoundly greater than us in our relationship. He stands above us as the Creator and sustainer. But this doesn't lessen the strength of our bond.

Scripture teaches us about friendship. One verse says that a friend loves us at all times (Proverbs 17:17). Another passage says that God is a friend more loyal than a brother (Proverbs 18:24). These verses highlight the enduring loyalty and unconditional love of genuine friendship from God.

Another proverb tells us we can trust the wounds of a friend (Proverbs 27:6). This means we can receive difficult truth when given in love from a friend—especially when that friend is God.

Through Jesus, we see the pinnacle of divine friendship. He sacrifices himself for us. He dies so that we might live. This is the epitome of love (John 15:13). Through his sacrificial death on the cross— to pay the penalty for all the wrong things we have done—he redeems us and makes us right with Papa.

When we accept Jesus's no-strings-attached gift of salvation, we receive eternal life. This eternal life starts today in this world and continues into the next when we die.

After teaching them this truth, Jesus elevates his disciples from the status of servants. In short, he calls them his friends (John 15:14–15). So, too, with us today.

From this, we can easily see Jesus as our friend. Yet the Father sent Jesus to us (Galatians 4:4). This shows Father God as our friend too. And they both sent us the Holy Spirit (John 14:26 and John 15:26). This makes him our friend as well.

Though most people naturally gravitate toward one part of the Trinity (Father, Son, or Holy Spirit) over the other two parts, we must realize that all three parts of God exist as our friend.

Just as God exists in relationship (as Father, Son, and Holy Spirit), he longs to be in relationship with us, his creation. How wonderful—how awesomely amazing—that God wants to be our friend.

With God as our friend, we communicate, share life, and spend time together.

Questions:

- How well do we do at accepting God as our friend?
- What can we do to be a better friend to God?

EMBRACE MORE METAPHORS

For the final part of our exploration of metaphors that reveal God to us, we looked at six images that reflect the godhead's character.

We start at the beginning with God as our Creator. We also acknowledge him as Lord and Judge. He is our consuming fire. He rightly stands as our Master and wants to be our friend.

Questions:

- Which of these six metaphors of God do we most connect with? What can we do to embrace it more fully?

- Which of these metaphors do we most struggle with? What steps should we take to lessen our apprehension?

WRAPPING UP

W e opened this book with the fable of the six blind men and the elephant. Each of these men has a partial understanding of what an elephant is like. Each one makes a correct, although highly narrow, conclusion. These observations are insightful, but they're also limited.

When we combine them, we can see that the elephant is like a wall, a tree, and a spear. It's like a snake, a fan, and a whip. Through these, we get a fuller picture of an elephant's characteristics. Clarity emerges. Yet even with this, we still have a composite image that falls far short. If you've ever seen a drawing of an elephant with these six components, it's quite humorous because it's completely inadequate to reveal what an elephant is really like.

In parallel fashion, we covered thirty-two illustrations of various facets of God and his character. There may be more, but this is a great start. These are like pieces of a puzzle. When we connect them, a bigger, fuller picture of God materializes. Then, how we relate to him emerges as well.

From these thirty-two images of God, we understand more of who he is, but it's still an incomplete picture. It's partial. But it's the best we can do with what we know at this time. These give us a more inclusive view of God, a more holistic understanding of who he is and what he is about. This helps us to relate to him on a more effective basis.

Paul explains this dilemma with a powerful image of his own: a mirror. At the present, it's like we're looking into a mirror. What we see is a reflection. Later we will see God face to face. Now we know in part. Later we will know in full (1 Corinthians 13:12). What a glorious day that will be.

Consider some of the key metaphors we

covered that highlight who God is and reveal truth about our relationship with him.

On a basic level, he is the potter, and we are the clay; he is the vine, and we are the branches; he is a hen, and we are his chicks. Now consider three higher level metaphors: He is our shepherd, and we are his sheep; he is our Master, and we are his servants; he is our Father, and we are his children. Even more significant, we have the imagery of friendship between God and us. Ultimately, we see Jesus as the bridegroom and we are his bride.

But we must embrace these word pictures of God as a comprehensive understanding and not take them in isolation. This would cause us to reach harmful conclusions. For example, if we only looked at God as a potter, with us as his clay, we could assume we have no control over what happens. We might conclude that we lack free will and are subject to whatever he wants to do to us. Though this carries an element of truth, it's only part of the fuller picture.

With God as our potter, we may see him as sovereign. Yet if we think of the Almighty only as a sovereign God, our prayers can become wimpy—even unneeded. I've heard these types of petitions.

"God, if it's your will, work these things out according to your timing, Amen."

A request like this, however, doesn't ask for much. It doesn't stretch our faith. It risks nothing. How will we even know if God answers it? Whatever the outcome, we could just shrug our shoulders and say, "Well, I guess it was God's will."

An alternate prayer might be, "God, I believe this is what you want me to do. Give me strength to move forward in faith. Grant me favor as I meet with people to bring it about. Please allow me to accomplish it this week. Thank you for hearing my prayer and for the answers you will provide."

At least, that's how I might present it.

Prayers like this risk much because they might not be answered the way we want. But the risk we take will grow our faith. Our understanding of God increases; it deepens. Our perspective of our Lord and our relationship with him becomes fuller and more effective. That's not to say that sometimes prayers like this challenge us or make us doubt a little, but in working through them, we can grow. We must consider this as we pray.

In another example of the risk in taking one of these illustrations in isolation, consider God as our shepherd and us as his sheep. If we focus on it and think of ourselves only as sheep prone to make stupid mistakes and wander off, we'll probably do just that. Though it's true that we sometimes act like foolish sheep, it's only part of the picture of who we are in relation to God.

In this way, it's critical for us to embrace a more inclusive view of who God is and who we are in Him. These thirty-two illustrations will help us do just that.

Concluding Questions:

- Which of this book's analogies do you appreciate and like the best? How does it encourage you?
- What other metaphors for God do you like? Why?
- Which of these word pictures challenge you the most? Do any make you mad? What should you do to consider them from a fresh perspective?
- In this book, what have you learned about God? What have you learned about yourself?

- How has your faith grown? What's your next step?

If you liked *Elephant God*, please leave a review online. Your review will help others discover this book and encourage them to read it too.

Thank you.

FOR SMALL GROUPS, SUNDAY SCHOOL, AND CLASSES

Elephant God makes an ideal book for small groups, Sunday School, and classes. To prepare for the conversation, read the assigned section or sections. Then contemplate your response to the questions at the end of each chapter.

When you get together, discuss the questions as a group. The leader can use all the questions to guide your discussion, pick which ones to focus on, or add more.

Before beginning the discussion, pray as a group. Ask for Holy Spirit insight and clarity.

As you consider each chapter's questions:

- Look for how this can grow your understanding of God.

- Evaluate how this can expand your faith perspective.
- Consider what you need to change in how you relate to God.

End by asking God to help you apply what you've learned.

May God bless you on your faith journey with him.

ABOUT PETER DEHAAN

Peter DeHaan, PhD, wants to change the world one word at a time. His books and blog posts discuss God, the Bible, and church, geared toward spiritual seekers and church dropouts. Many people feel church has let them down, and Peter seeks to encourage them as they search for a place to belong.

But he's not afraid to ask tough questions or make religious people squirm. He's not trying to be provocative. Instead, he seeks truth, even if it makes people uncomfortable. Writing from a biblical worldview, Peter urges Christians to push past the status quo and reexamine how they practice their faith in every part of their lives.

Peter earned his doctorate, awarded with high distinction, from Trinity College of the Bible and Theological Seminary. He lives with his wife in beautiful Southwest Michigan and wrangles cross-word puzzles in his spare time.

A lifelong student of Scripture, Peter wrote the

1,000-page website ABibleADay.com to encourage people to explore the Bible, the greatest book ever written. His popular blog addresses biblical Christianity to build a faith that matters.

Read his blog, receive his newsletter, and learn more at PeterDeHaan.com.

BOOKS BY PETER DEHAAN

40-Day Bible Study Series

Dear Theophilus (the Gospel of Luke)

Acts Bible Study

Isaiah Bible Study

Minor Prophets Bible Study

Job Bible Study

Living Water (John)

Love Is Patient (1 and 2 Corinthians)

Revelation Bible Study

1, 2, & 3 John Bible Study

Hebrews Bible Study

James and Jude Bible Study

Matthew Bible Study

1 & 2 Peter Bible Study

Mark Bible Study

Romans Bible Study

Paul's Short Epistles Bible Study

Holiday Celebration Devotionals

The Advent of Jesus

The Passion of Jesus (Lent)

The Victory of Jesus (Easter)

The Ministry of Jesus

Thanksgiving with Jesus

New Year with Jesus

Bible Character Sketches Series

Women of the Bible

The Friends and Foes of Jesus

Old Testament Sinners and Saints

More Old Testament Sinners and Saints

Heroes and Heavies of the Apocrypha

200 Old Testament Sinners and Saints

Visiting Churches Series

52 Churches

The 52 Churches Workbook

More Than 52 Churches

The More Than 52 Churches Workbook

Visiting Online Church

Shopping for Church

Other Books

Jesus's Broken Church

Martin Luther's 95 Theses

The Christian Church's LGBTQ Failure

Bridging the Sacred-Secular Divide

Beyond Psalm 150

For the latest list of all Peter's books, go to PeterDeHaan.com/nonfiction.